THE SHAAR PRESS

THE JUDAICA IMPRINT
FOR THOUGHTFUL PEOPLE

SELF-IM-PROVE-MENT?

A
SHAAR
PRESS
PUBLICATION

OVERCOMING SELF-DEFEATING BEHAVIOR

— I'M JEWISH!

RABBI ABRAHAM J. TWERSKI, M.D.

Published by **SHAAR PRESS**
Distributed by MESORAH PUBLICATIONS, LTD.
4401 Second Avenue / Brooklyn, New York 11232 / (718) 921-9000

Distributed in Israel by SIFRIATI / A. GITLER BOOKS
4 Bilu Street / P.O.B. 14075 / Tel Aviv 61140

Distributed in Europe by J. LEHMANN HEBREW BOOKSELLERS
20 Cambridge Terrace / Gateshead, Tyne and Wear / England NE8 1RP

Distributed in Australia and New Zealand by GOLDS BOOK & GIFT SHOP
36 William Street / Balaclava 3183, Vic., Australia

Distributed in South Africa by KOLLEL BOOKSHOP
22 Muller Street / Yeoville 2198 / Johannesburg, South Africa

ISBN: 0-89906-583-X Hard Cover
ISBN: 0-89906-584-8 Paperback

Printed in the United States of America by Moriah Offset
Custom bound by Sefercraft, Inc. / 4401 Second Avenue / Brooklyn, N.Y. 11232

SELF-IM-PROVE-MENT? —I'M JEWISH!

Introduction

Does Everyone Need Self-improvement?

Yankel was engaged in doing something of questionable propriety on Shabbos. A passerby remarked, "Yankel, have you forgotten it is Shabbos?"

"I asked the Rabbi," Yankel said.

The man shrugged and left. Soon a second passerby made the same comment to Yankel and was given the same answer. The third passerby, upon hearing

Yankel's answer, asked, "And what did the Rabbi say?"'

"He said it's not allowed," Yankel said.

"Nu?"

"So I didn't listen to him," Yankel said.

It is not enough to know what the Torah says. We must listen too.

Torah writings teach that a person must constantly advance himself. Angels are created in a state of spiritual perfection, and they remain stationary. Man is created in a state of potential, and must continually progress.

There is a well-known story of R' Saadiah Gaon, who went incognito to an inn where he lodged. Shortly before R' Saadiah left, the innkeeper learned of his identity and apologized profusely. "Had I known who you were, I would have treated you with much greater respect."

The great sage began to weep. "Had I known the greatness of God yesterday the way I know it today, I would have worshipped Him altogether differently yesterday," he said.

The principle stated by R' Saadiah Gaon applies to all of us. Each day we should reach a higher spiritual level, which should make our status of the previous day appear inadequate.

But let us be honest with ourselves. We are far from the status of R' Saadiah Gaon, whose spiritual progress was akin to polishing a scintillating gem to further enhance its great beauty. Most of us are at a far more scaled-down status, comparable to an unpolished gem which requires major work before its luster becomes evident.

At whatever level we may be, we can all benefit from self-improvement. Most of us know this in theory, but it is not always translated into practice. Some of us have lifestyles that are frankly self-defeating, and that cause us to regress rather than to progress.

Let us look at some of the more common self-defeating behaviors, and apply the Torah principles to reverse these patterns, so that we may achieve spiritual progress.

L ife, liberty, and the pursuit of happiness; these are clearly the drives that motivate human beings. These opening words of the Declaration of Independence have inspired people to strive for freedom and to throw off the tyranny of enslavement to despots. Yet, if one observes the human condition, it becomes apparent that rather than striving toward life, liberty, and the pursuit of happiness, many people seem to be heading in the opposite direction, behaving in a manner that jeopardizes their lives, subjects them to enslavement, and results in misery. If you were to ask such an individual why he is abandoning life, liberty, and the pursuit of happiness in favor of their polar opposites, he will look at you with dismay, because in his opinion, he is indeed striving for life, liberty, and the pursuit of happiness. While to all objective observers the person is engaged in self-defeating behavior, he is not aware of this. To the contrary, he views his behavior as self-enhancing rather than self-defeating.

There are various types of self-defeating behaviors. For example, some people have a lifestyle that is characterized by pervasive anger. They are always angry at someone or something, and seem to be constantly on the lookout for a target on whom to vent their wrath. We have coined the term, "He is walking around with a chip on his shoulder," to describe this type of person. It is evident to everyone that this attitude results in anything but happiness, and it may also bring about high blood pressure with the incipient dangers of stroke and heart disease. Often the person appears to be unable to free himself from this attitude. In other words, this person, whom we may call a "rage-aholic," is in reality striving for the opposite of life, liberty, and the pursuit of happiness. If you were to ask him, however, what he expects to accomplish with his rage-aholism, you will discover that he feels that he is indeed striving to achieve the coveted goals, and that his rage is simply the result of the fact that everyone and everything in the world is standing in the way of his achieving life, liberty, and the pursuit of happiness.

Much the same is true of a person who may not manifest rage, but has a lifestyle of moping, whining, and being chronically depressed. There are also many people who have adapted themselves to a lifestyle of loneliness, isolation, and alienation from people. There are some people who are chronic procrastinators, constantly delaying life instead of living it, and never even getting around to life, liberty, and the pursuit of happiness. Closely related to, if not identical with procrastination is indolence, whose self-defeating nature is vividly described by King Solomon. "Yet a little sleep, a little more slumber, a little folding of the hands to rest, and your poverty will stalk you" (*Proverbs* 24:33). These are just several examples of lifestyles that can be referred to as "self-defeating"; i.e., if we assume that people wish to achieve, life, liberty, and the pursuit of happiness, these lifestyles essentially prevent achievement of these goals.

While some self-defeating lifestyles may be more subtle, there are some self-defeating patterns that are quite obvious, the most striking of these being *alcoholism*. In this scenario you may have a highly intelligent person, well endowed with skills that could earn him a genuine measure of life, liberty, and happiness, yet he seems hellbent on ruining his health, making himself miserable, and he appears helplessly and hopelessly enslaved by his alcoholism. The same holds true for other addictions, notably drugs, food, gambling, and smoking. In each case the person involved will swear that he is in pursuit of life, liberty, and happiness, while his addictive behavior is clearly defeating any and all possibilities of achieving these objectives.

There are many factors that are common to all these self-defeating behaviors. These, however, are so pronounced in alcoholism that even the prophets in the Scriptures often use alcoholism as representative of all self-defeating lifestyles, as when the prophet says, "They are drunk but not with wine, and they blunder but not with ale" (Isaiah 29:9).

My clinical experience with treating alcoholics has substantiated this. My observation of a variety of self-defeating behaviors has shown them to be essentially similar to alcoholism, although there may or may not be a particular substance involved, such as a chemical or food. Rage-aholism is no less self-defeating than alcoholism, and this is true of other lifestyles as well such as alienation, depression, and procrastination.

This position is more than validated by Rabbi Samson Raphael Hirsch in his commentary on the Book of Proverbs. In regard to pleasure-indulgence and greed, Rabbi Hirsch says,

> As long as a craving or an appetite is still young, we can easily subdue it by granting it only what is admissible, and thus keep it under control for the rest of our lives. But if we allow it more than its due from the beginning, and spoil it by over-indulgence, it will soon cease to be submissive and will make ever-growing demands upon us. . .One craving that has been

humored acquires many companions and engenders many appetites. Once these dominate a person, he will find his ruin in a debauched way of life. Were we to eat only when hungry, we would not miss delicacies. We like such unnecessary stimuli to our appetite only because we eat beyond our actual need; and this may easily lead to harmful pampering.

Entertainment, wine, and oil, may not be objectionable in themselves, but we are not to become their companions. The love of enjoyments and the pleasures of luxury ultimately leads to impoverishment. *What is worse, the character of our thinking and behavior toward our peers is dangerously affected by indulgence in wine.* . . .People who become dehumanized by excessive eating and drinking finally waste whatever they possess and become unable to reacquire what they need. . .

Greed is even more ruinous than pleasure seeking. While pleasure has a saturation point, and an excess of indulgence finally makes it impossible to tolerate more, greed is insatiable. To a man who has been unable to check it, it becomes a passion against which he remains totally defenseless [and he is subsequently overwhelmed by the need to take possession of everything and anything within his reach.

However,] there is one limit to greed: [The avaricious individual instigates a] self-inflicted one of arousing opposition on the part of competitors [who curb his powers of acquisition]. As for a cure, however, greed has only one remedy: *faith in G-d*. Only someone who thinks that his and his family's destiny is dependent entirely upon himself and his own abilities can become a victim of unlimited greediness (*From the Wisdom of Mishle*, Feldheim, 1976, pgs. 223-227).

These few remarks by this great Torah scholar relate as well to all self-defeating behaviors, for which alcoholism can serve as a paradigm.

Having observed that many alcoholics have recovered and have abandoned their self-defeating behavior, and that the methods they used to accomplish this have been equally successful in other self-defeating addictive disorders, such as drug addiction, eating disorders, and compulsive gambling, it was only logical to see whether these methods might also be constructively applied to other counterproductive lifestyles, even those which do not involve the use of a particular substance. I have reason to believe that this is indeed the case. If we follow the prophet's direction and use alcoholism as a prototype of self-defeating behaviors, we may successfully apply those techniques that have been effective in overcoming alcoholism to prevail over other ill-considered behaviors. Let me share with you how I found the recovery program for alcoholism to be helpful, and the effective techniques which can be derived from this program.

A bit later I will call attention to the reasons why the group approach toward surmounting self-defeating behaviors is effective. However, I have found that there is often considerable resistance among Jews to participate in a group program that is directed toward personality problems. Much of this resistance is related to an ingrained cultural trait which fosters concealment of all personal problems, which remain carefully guarded secrets within the immediate family. In some instances this is due to the time-honored practice of *shidduchim*, whereby couples meet as a result of matchmaking, and a prospective candidate for a *shidduch* (match) may be disqualified because of an incidence or a history of illness, especially a behavioral disorder, within the family. In those situations where a couple has already made a commitment and the skeleton in the closet is subsequently discovered, the latter is often overlooked according to the Scriptural observation that "Love covers an abundance of faults" (*Proverbs* 10:12). When couples are introduced only after a background check has been made, the existence of a defect within the family may ruin the chances of a match. Understandably, troubles, especially personal problems, within the family are hushed up to safeguard the children's opportunity for marriage.

This is a fact of life, albeit an unfortunate one. It is not unusual for me to receive a call requesting help for someone who has an alcohol, drug, or gambling problem, with the calling party saying, "I can't tell you my name, and I hope you will understand." Yes, I understand, but I do not agree.

Frequently I am contacted by distraught families

who are seeking a kosher psychiatric hospital or treatment center, particularly one where the patient would not be exposed to influences that are incompatible with Torah and which might undermine the person's Yiddishkeit, especially when one is in a fragile emotional state. No such facility exists at present, and due to the penchant for secrecy, it is unlikely that one will ever exist. Many people will be reluctant to admit a family member to a facility where there are many Jews for fear they may be recognized and the family will be stigmatized.

I have said that I understand but I do not agree, and this is because I have found concealment to be futile. Many families are shocked to discover that their secret has already been exposed, and that while they were oblivious to what was transpiring, others had already noted that there was a problem, and had come to an accurate conclusion concerning the nature of the problem. Furthermore, the natural course of addictive conditions is such that unless they are brought under control by appropriate treatment, they will progress to a point where concealment is no longer feasible, and the exposure that will occur will be far worse than that which might have come about as a result of treatment.

For example, one family tried to conceal their son's addictive gambling, which had resulted in his issuing fraudulent checks and borrowing money on other's credit cards. To avoid the possible scandal and the subsequent blackening of the family name, they paid off the debts and elicited a promise that he would never gamble again, a promise which was of no substance, because addicts do not keep promises. Several years later the amount of money owed was beyond the family's ability to repay, and the infractions of the law could not be covered up, with the resulting exposure being far more damaging to all concerned.

I will return to the need for a group approach a bit later, but first let me tell you about the most popular recovery program and how its methods can be adopted.

In the mid-1930s, two men joined forces to begin what eventually became the single largest and most effective recovery program for people with alcohol addiction: Alcoholics Anonymous. In the decades that followed, this program was adapted to help people with other compulsive behaviors, such as narcotic addiction, eating disorders, and compulsive gambling.

I initially made contact with the Twelve Step program of AA in the line of treating alcoholism. It then became evident to me that a program that has such wide applications and is effective in treating various other conditions cannot be specific for any single problem. The common denominator is that it is effective in overcoming self-defeating lifestyles, regardless of what the particular type of self-destructive activity may be. It further became evident that the salutary results are due to a change in lifestyle rather than the elimination of any one or even a group of symptoms.

I became enamored of AA for several reasons. Primarily, it was my first (and only) contact with a program that practices true equality. In AA, who you are and how much you own are not given the slightest consideration. There is no leadership position to entice those who are vulnerable to lust for power, and there is no way in which anyone who wields power by virtue of position or wealth can have any special privileges.

I know of no other organization, charitable, secular, or religious, where major donors do not exert an influence. Synagogues and churches have payrolls and expenses to meet, and possibly huge mortgage payments. They are dependent on the contributions of the membership for survival. A member who is a pillar of support of the congregation and whose annual contribution constitutes a significant portion of the budget is very likely to receive special treatment. The organization simply cannot afford the risk of his leaving as a result of becoming angry because his feathers were ruffled. Other members, who may be every bit as dear to the rabbi or officers, but whose support is not as vital, may not be given the same preferential treatment as the major philanthropist.

But isn't everyone equal before G-d? But G-d is G-d. And though we must do our utmost to emulate him, for us mere mortals there is no escaping the fact that while everyone is equal, some are more equal than others.

How refreshing it was when I discovered that in AA it makes no difference who you are and how much you possess. Once a person enters the meeting room, he/she is a human being in distress, desiring help, or a grateful person who wishes to maintain his/her recovery and share their good fortune with others.

I once came into a meeting room and saw two of my recovering patients sitting next to each other, sharing a conversation. Nancy was a very wealthy woman, who was no doubt driven to the meeting by her chauffeur in a luxury car. Edith, on the other hand, had to have an attendance slip signed by the group secretary so that her bus fare could be refunded by welfare, otherwise she could not afford to come to meetings. These two women were poles apart socially, but completely equal within the confines of that room. Nancy's wealth could not acquire any privileges for her. Indeed, Nancy might have needed Edith's help to stay sober. The fact that each human being is treated as an equal in every way was a phenomenon that I had not and have not encountered elsewhere, and this would have been enough to endear the program to me.

To add to this, I discovered a willingness to help another person, to a degree that is rarely found elsewhere. There are of course many people who are benevolent and charitable, and who will give of themselves, but sometimes even these commendable traits have their limitations.

Imagine being awakened at 2:00 a.m. on a snowy, freezing winter night, and asked to go to the home of a total stranger, because the latter has called for help. One gets dressed, struggles to get the car started in sub-zero weather, and drives through a blizzard, replete with hazardous snow and sleet, in the full knowledge that when he finally arrives at the home of the supplicant who may be intoxicated, he may find the latter to have had an abrupt change of mind. If he is lucky, he gets the door slammed in his face, or if less fortunate, he can be thrown down the stairs by an irate intoxicated individual.

All this notwithstanding, one responds to the call for help, and on returning home will phone the dispatcher to thank him for the opportunity to have been of help.

A topflight attorney, with whom one must schedule an appointment several weeks in advance and pay a hefty fee, responded to one such call at midnight, and remained with the caller for four hours, finally gaining his consent to be driven to the hospital for treatment. Professionally, these hours during the business day would have been worth a king's ransom, but the attorney gave of his time willingly and gratefully during the wee hours of the night, because of a commitment to be of help to a person in distress. This, too, endeared the program to me.

Although I initially attended Twelve Step meetings to learn more about the people I had to treat, I soon found that I could gain much from these programs for myself, and I have been a staunch advocate of them, as being effective and helping people adjust to the many stresses and distresses of life.

Nevertheless, many Jews, especially those who are Torah observant, have said that inasmuch as recovery from any addictive condition requires a change in one's lifestyle, why should they adopt a Twelve Step program? Certainly there can be nothing finer and more effective than a Torah-true lifestyle. While the Twelve Step program may indeed be necessary for those who are not familiar with Torah and *mitzvos*, those who live according to the principles of Torah should have no need for anything else.

I cannot possibly disagree with this. There is no lifestyle that can equal that of Torah observance. It is common practice that if one acquires a complex apparatus, one reads the manufacturer's instructions to know how to operate it and maintain it properly. Deviating from these instructions can result in mal-function and damage to the apparatus. Inasmuch as the Torah was given to us by the Creator, it constitutes the "Manufacturer's instructions," and by adhering to these instructions, one should avoid any and all mal-adjustments. Therefore, although I am a strong advocate of the Twelve Step programs, I must respond pos-itively to those who argue that living a Torah-true life will obviate the need for any other program. I have therefore agreed to respond to the requests of those who wish to have a Torah program for recovery, rather than a Twelve Step program.

We must understand, however, that a Torah program requires total compliance in order for it to be effective. One cannot be partially observant, whether fifty percent or ninety-five percent, and expect favorable results. Moses begins his review of the Torah commandments by stating "Do not add to them and do not detract from them" (*Deuteronomy* 4:2). If you have a lock whose combination is 6-1-3, it will not open if you dial 6-1-2. Furthermore, Torah observance requires absolute adherence to all *mitzvos* and injunctions of rabbinic origin, and living according to *mussar* (ethics) as well as *halachah* (formal law). One cannot consider oneself to be truly observant if one neglects *mussar*, even if one complies with *halachah*. Halfway measures avail us nothing. It is not easy for a person to recognize that he has been living a self-defeating lifestyle. The psychological mechanism of *denial* can blind a person to even the most obvious self-destructive behavior. Rabbi Chaim Shmulevitz in his lectures on ethics (5732:7) cites the Scriptures which relate the story of Chiel who rebuilt Jericho in defiance of the curse uttered by Joshua that whoever would re-establish the city would incur the loss of his children (*Joshua* 6:26). When Chiel began to rebuild Jericho his oldest child died, and his children continued to perish as he proceeded with the construction, until his youngest and last surviving child died as he completed the city gates (*I Kings* 16:34). Although he certainly loved his children, Chiel was oblivious to what was transpiring before his very eyes. He knew of the curse and he saw his children dying, but could not associate the two. That is how formidable *denial* can be.

In the very same lecture, Rabbi Shmulevitz cites a Midrash about a family who was very distraught because their father was a drunkard. One day they saw a decidedly drunk person staggering and wallowing in the mud, who was being jeered and stoned by children. They ran home to fetch their father to witness this scene, in the hope that this would deter him from drinking. "Look, Father," they said, "this is exactly what happens to you when you drink." The father bent over the fallen drunkard and whispered in his ear, "My good man, where did you get such fine wine?" (*Tanhuma, Shmini*). Rabbi Shmulevitz states that as with Chiel, this alcoholic was oblivious to the self-destructive nature of his misconduct.

How do self-defeating behaviors develop? What happens is that a person has an experience, either an action or an attitude, that results in relief from distress or an apparent solution to a problem. He then continues to apply this action or attitude to subsequent distressful or problematic situations, even though it is now inappropriate and is not effective in these new situations. The Talmud points this out by saying, "Every falsehood that does not begin with a bit of truth does not endure" (*Sotah* 49a). The first experience contains "a bit of truth"; i.e., it worked in that particular instance, and the person then repeats and perpetuates this behavior in the expectation that it will work again, but this time it is totally false and ineffective. The *yetzer hara*, however, is cunning in deluding a person to interpret falsehood as truth.

For example, a person may find himself in a difficult situation, and delays doing something about it. While he is dawdling, the situation somehow corrects itself, which is, of course, not at all that uncommon. However, the person draws the erroneous conclusion that by delaying action, problems will go away, and then tries to apply this postponing tactic to all subsequent problems, thereby becoming a chronic procrastinator. If the first delay would not have had a favorable outcome, he possibly would not have become a procrastinator, but as the Talmud points out, because it proved effective initially, it tends to be perpetuated.

Similarly, a person who feels very tense and takes a drink may find that his anxiety disappears and that he suffered no ill effects. His conclusion: Alcohol is a tranquilizer that has no harmful side-effects. When subsequent tensions arise, he returns to what worked once, and although this time the drinking may have undesirable consequences, he cannot recognize this. On the same order, when a frustrated mother shouts at the children who are misbehaving at the table, and they suddenly become silent and behave better, she has discovered that anger works. However, continued attempts to control her children's conduct with anger eventually become ineffective and even counterproductive, but the mother may not recognize this. Or again, a person found that by spending a few additional hours at the office he was able to earn extra money, and eventually becomes a workaholic. The "law of diminishing returns" soon sets in, so that he becomes less productive instead of more productive. The first "bit of truth" set the scene for adoption of a pattern of falsehood.

There is reason to believe that this is how some eating disorders arise. The tiny infant's first experience of discomfort is hunger, and when he eats, the discomfort disappears. This initial experience is impressed on the mind, and later in life, when the person feels distress, he may turn to what once proved effective to relieve distress: food. Or, as may often happen early in life, parents feed young children and show their pleasure when the child eats. This is especially common in Jewish families where *ess, ess, mein ziss kind* (eat, eat, my sweet child) is a frequent parental refrain. The impression the child may be left with is that one gets the approval of parents or significant others by eating. Later in life, the person may turn to food as if eating would again gain the approval he seeks from his boss, friends, or spouse. Rationally, this makes no sense whatsoever, but the unconscious mind does not operate by rational thought. Rather, it tends to apply methods that once worked to situations where they are totally inappropriate and even counterproductive.

There are many situations where a particular action or attitude has a favorable result; i.e., there is a "bit of truth." The misconception occurs when one tries to duplicate this favorable result, and although it is not forthcoming, one is duped by the *yetzer hara* into believing that it has worked again.

For example, the first drinking episode may have provided relief from tension without any untoward effects. The next time a person tries to drink himself out of an unpleasant situation the result is negative, and his problem remains unresolved. Instead of recognizing that alcohol does not solve problems, he is misled by the *yetzer hara* which tells him, "Of course alcohol gave you relief. The reason the problem remained unsolved or worsened is because so-and-so (the boss, the son, the daughter, the parents, the wife, the customer, the competitor) ruined everything for you." The *yetzer hara* teaches a person to project blame for failure onto others, but to retain the false impression that alcohol is a solution to problems. This is true of virtually every self-defeating behavior. As the Talmud says, it begins with a "bit of truth," and the *yetzer hara* exploits this "bit of truth" to deceive a person.

Those who have come to the realization that a change in lifestyle is necessary have not come to this conclusion easily. Invariably, they have tried various and sundry methods to overcome their problem. People with a chemical dependency have taken pledges and sworn never to use it again. They have eliminated alcohol from the home. One young physician, addicted to narcotics, knew that he was jeopardizing his career, and when he had the urge to use drugs he would take out a photograph of his wife and infant son whom he loved so dearly, and say to himself, "You will not do this to them." At times he saturated the picture with his tears, only to put it away and then inject narcotics. People with compulsive overeating have taken appetite suppressants and gone on a variety of miracle diets, often losing excess weight, only to regain the lost poundage plus some. It is only after all these efforts have failed and they find themselves profoundly distressed that they recognize that they are powerless over their condition and that their lives have become unmanageable. It is then that they are ready to take the difficult but effective path of changing their lifestyle.

It is little wonder that people look for easier methods. Changing one's lifestyle is very difficult. Just try and make a slight change in your regular way of doing things, and you will discover that it is distinctly uncomfortable to do so. For example, if you customarily wear your wrist watch on your left hand, put it on your right hand. You will discover that you are conscious of its being there, whereas this was not so when it was on the left wrist. Or fold your arms over your chest, and note whether you do it left over right or vice versa. Now do it the other way, and you will note that it feels distinctly awkward. If such minute, insignificant changes can result in feeling strange and can cause one to go back to his usual way of doing things, just image how distressful it must be to make major changes in one's lifestyle.

The forces of habit and temptation are so strong that the Talmud states it is impossible for a person to triumph over them without Divine assistance. "A person's *yetzer hara* (natural physical inclinations) grows stronger every day, and if G-d were not to help a person, he could never overcome it" (*Succah* 52a). It is clear then, that if one is to escape from a self-defeating lifestyle, one cannot do it on his own. Obviously, one must make a maximum effort. "One should not rely on miracles" (*Pesachim* 64b), and having faith and trust in G-d does not mean that one may sit in the passenger seat and ask G-d to do the driving. However, while we must do everything reasonable within our means to set our lives straight, we must invoke the help of G-d, for without it we cannot succeed.

There is a story about a person who, beginning weeks before Passover, laboriously cleaned his house for the festival, and cleansed his kitchen from *chometz* to the point of surgical sterility. On the last day of Passover he discovered that in the well from which he had drawn his water during all of Passover there was a loaf of bread floating on the surface. Broken hearted, he asked his rabbi why he had fallen victim to this transgression, especially since he had exerted so much effort and energy to avoid *chometz*.

The rabbi explained, "The prevalence of *chometz* all year round makes it physically impossible to eliminate it totally by unaided human effort. You tried very hard indeed, but you forgot to pray to G-d to make your efforts successful. Had you prayed for

Divine assistance, then all the work you had done would have been blessed. By failing to pray, you indicated that you thought you could do it yourself, and so you were shown that you were wrong."

For prayer to be effective, it must be said with *kavannah* (concentration). In the morning prayers we ask G-d to spare us from various evils, including the temptation of the *yetzer hara*, but too often we say the words without putting our hearts fully into them. Just mumbling the words is not quality prayer and is unlikely to be effective. The prophet is very intolerant of this kind of prayer, and his words are penetrating. "This people has approached Me with their mouths, praising Me with their lips, while their hearts remain distant. Their reverence for Me is one of habit and routine" (*Isaiah* 29:13). When a person is, G-d forbid, stricken with disease, and stands before the Ark praying for the Divine intervention necessary for recovery, he does so with great *kavannah* because he is pleading for life itself. That is the kind of *kavannah* necessary for our prayers to be spared from the *yetzer hara* to be effective. We must desire this salvation with all our hearts and be ready to go to any lengths to obtain it.

Nothing can be achieved without Divine help. The Talmud states, "What should a person do to become wise? He must increase the time he spends in Torah study and decrease the amount of time he devotes to making money." The Talmud then notes that some people have acted accordingly, yet did not achieve wisdom and states that this is because they did not pray to G-d for wisdom. While prayer without study will not result in acquiring wisdom, neither will study without prayer for Divine assistance accomplish this (*Niddah* 70b).

As we noted, prayer for Divine assistance will be effective only after one has made maximum efforts on his own. The problem is that sometimes our own efforts may be on the wrong track; i.e., we wish to do what is right, and we may think that what we are doing is right, yet we are being counterproductive. If one needs to head east to reach one's destination, but because of a poor sense of direction one heads west instead, one will only get further away. We need to know that what we are doing is indeed right.

I grasped an important insight about *teshuvah* by overhearing a conversation between a veteran of many years of sobriety who reprimanded a newcomer to the program for not attending an AA meeting. The young man defended himself by saying that the weather was terrible: Cold, blizzard conditions, icy streets.

"Would this weather have kept you back from going for a drink when you craved it?" the sponsor asked. The latter had to admit that he would have gone for a drink in any kind of weather.

"If you do not want sobriety badly enough to make the same effort to get it that you would have made to get a drink, then you are not yet ready for recovery," the sponsor said.

This is the acid test of quality *teshuvah*. Are you ready to invest the same efforts in the observance of Torah and *mitzvos* that you did when you transgressed them?

For a judge to make a just decision, he must be free of bribery. The Torah states that a judge who accepts a bribe cannot possibly be objective (*Deuteronomy* 16:19), and this also holds true for all judgments we make concerning our actions as individuals. If we want things to be a certain way, we will see them that way. Our capacity to rationalize is nothing less than uncanny. One recovering alcoholic told me, "In all the years that I drank, I never took a drink unless I decided that it was the right and proper thing to do at the time." As King Solomon says in the *Book of Proverbs,* (12:15), "The ways of the fool appear appropriate in his eyes" and a person is indeed foolish if he deceives himself.

In *Michtav M'Eliyahu*, Rabbi Dessler states that if someone consults the *Shulchan Aruch* (Code of Law) to see whether it is permissible to play chess on Shabbos, it is a foregone conclusion what he wants. Unless the *Shulchan Aruch* explicitly forbids it, he is left to his own resources to make a judgment, and it is very likely that his decision will be influenced by his desires. There are many things we desire in life, and all of these have the capacity to distort our decision-making power in favor of satisfying those desires.

What then is the solution? The answer is provided by the Talmud: "Negate your will before the will of G-d, and make His will your will" (*Ethics of the Fathers*

2:4). Turn your life over to the Divine will, and set your own desires aside, because otherwise you will be drawn to erroneous conclusions and possibly self-destructive behavior, without recognizing them as such.

If a person has overcome denial and has realized that his behavior has been self-defeating, he should be willing to accept that his own preferences have been misleading. King Solomon repeatedly exhorts us to be aware of the cunning of the *yetzer hara*, which makes things appear desirable, and blinds us to the devastation they may cause. How beautifully and succinctly he phrases it: "The bird that sees the bait is unaware of the trap that will capture it" (*Proverbs* 1:17), and again, "There is a way which may appear proper to a person, yet it leads only to death" (*Ibid.* 14:12). When one's experiences have demonstrated that his own will is totally unreliable, an intelligent person will adopt a will other than his own. And what better will can one adopt other than the Divine will?

But that only leads us to a further question. How am I to know what is the Divine will? Granted, the Torah-observant person has the *Shulchan Aruch* as his guide, which indicates which things are permissible and which things are prohibited. The *Shulchan Aruch* is an excellent and reliable guide for those issues with which it deals. But what about those myriad items that are not addressed specifically in the *Shulchan Aruch*? What about emotional and psychological issues? What guidelines are there in these areas?

There are two ways to deal with this, and we

should utilize both. First, the Talmud states: "Accept a teacher upon yourself." (*Ethics of the Fathers* 1:6), someone who knows more than you, someone who can address your problem objectively. Secondly, learn the great works on spirituality and study them diligently. The quotations cited from the *Book of Proverbs* indicate that it is a text on spirituality *par excellence*. There are many fine later works on spirituality, and perhaps the most authoritative and widely acclaimed is *Path of the Just* by Rabbi Moshe Chaim Luzatto, which is the primer for spirituality, and which is to the soul what oxygen is to the body. As the author indicates, this is a book which should be re-read many times.

Man cannot hope to reach an understanding of G-d or what it is that G-d desires by exercise of his intellect alone. Our understanding of G-d and His will is based on revealed teachings, beginning with those given to Moses and later to the prophets. The saintly sages of the Talmud received the oral tradition from their forebears, and were Divinely inspired to interpret the Scriptures.

Based on these sources, Torah scholars throughout the ages have given us our concept of G-d. They have interpreted the verse "Know the G-d of your father and serve Him" (*I Chronicles* 28:9) to mean that our concept of G-d is two-fold. There is the acceptance of the belief in G-d based on our *Mesorah*, the transmission from generation to generation originating with the Revelation at Sinai, and there is also a need to "know" G-d; i.e., to develop a concept about G-d, in full recognition that the human mind cannot possible understand Him.

As set forth by Luzatto and other ethicists, the goal of the Jew is attainment of spirituality. As I pointed out in my book *I'd Like to Call for Help, But I Don't Know the Number* (Pharos Books, 1991), spirituality is comprised of all those features that are uniquely human; i.e., that distinguish man from other forms of life. These are: (1) greater intellect; (2) the capacity to learn from the history of the past; (3) the capacity to think about the purpose of life; (4) the capacity to think of self-improvement; (5) the capacity to make salutary changes in oneself; (6) the capacity to think about future consequences of one's actions; (7) the capacity to delay gratification; and (8) the capacity to make truly free moral decisions. These eight features constitute *generic* spirituality. For the Torah-observant person, the purpose of life is dictated by the Torah, as explained in the writings of Luzatto, other ethicists, and the Chassidic masters, and consists of achieving a oneness with G-d (*Deuteronomy* 11:22).

The need for a spiritual guide cannot be overemphasized. Rabbi Yisroel of Salant states that the most difficult disposition to overcome is one which a person erroneously assumes to be the Divine will. Other personal desires can more easily be set aside, but if someone erroneously believes that what he is doing is for the greater glory of G-d, this conviction is most difficult to thwart.

Virtually every work on ethics addresses the need for *cheshbon hanefesh*, a thorough personal inventory of one's thoughts and actions. It is told of one of the *tzaddikim* that each night he would write down the events of the day, and when he found that he had done things which he considered improper, he would weep with regret until the tears washed away the recording of the sin. Perhaps this intense piety is a bit beyond the grasp of most people, but one can at least do the first part; i.e., make an accounting of everything he has done, and see which things need correction.

The term *cheshbon hanefesh* literally means an account of the spirit, and the word "account" should be taken in its commercial sense. If one was to be interested in acquiring a business, one would ask for a *cheshbon,* an accurate account which reflects the status of the business. If one were to look only at the negative side of the ledger, i.e., accounts payable, one might come to a grossly erroneous conclusion and assume that the business was failing. It is important also to consider the positive side of the ledger, i.e. the assets, the accounts receivable, and the merchandise in stock. It may turn out that although the business has some liabilities, it is indeed highly profitable and well worth acquiring.

It is thus a mistake to think that an inventory consists of only the mistakes or wrongs one has done. This would give a person a distorted perspective and a feeling of dejection and possibly one of despair. It is equally important to have an awareness of the positive aspects of one's behavior and character. The great ethicist, Rabbi Yeruchem Levovitz, said that a person who is unaware of his defects is certainly in a sad state, because he does not know what amends he must make in himself. However, a person who is oblivious of his character assets and virtues is much worse off, because he is unaware of the tools that he possesses wherewith he can make spiritual progress and the necessary salutary changes in himself.

It is understandable that a person may wish to remain unaware of his defects, but why would anyone have difficulty in accepting his own character assets? I dealt with this topic at some length in *Let Us Make Man* (CIS 1987) and in *Life's Too Short* (St. Martin's Press 1995). There are many reasons why a person might have low self-esteem and have developed a negative self-image in childhood, which then persists into maturity and often throughout his entire lifetime. An individual with a distorted self-perception tends to see himself as though he would be looking through the wrong end of a telescope: tiny, inadequate, and worthless. This distorted perception is most deplorable, since it often results in the erroneous conclusion that he lacks the necessary skills to cope satisfactorily with the challenges of life, and this may be a major reason why a person may seek to escape from reality instead of coping with it. Of course, one of the most common methods of escape from reality is by rendering oneself oblivious or insensitive to it by means of mind-altering chemicals. It is also possible that procrastination and indolence may have their origin in the feeling "What's the use in trying? I cannot succeed anyway."

There is a natural resistance to damaging something which one recognizes as being valuable and beautiful. People with a healthy self-esteem are therefore far less likely to do things that are injurious to themselves; hence a healthy self-esteem is a bulwark against self-defeating behaviors.

Some people confuse self-esteem with vanity and believe that for a person to be humble he must think poorly about himself. The error of such reasoning should be obvious, and it was best formulated by the ethicist Rabbi Leib Chasman, who said that a person who does not recognize his character assets is not humble, but rather a fool. The truly humble person is aware that he has skills and talents, that they are gifts from G-d, and that he must utilize them to the fullest. Since they are capabilities that were given to him, he has no right to boast about them, and the realization of how little he has yet achieved with his G-d-given talents should make him truly humble.

There is yet another possible reason for a person to resist awareness of his abilities, which became evident to me when a young woman of twenty-four entered the hospital for treatment of alcoholism and requested psychological testing.

"Why do you want psychological tests?" I asked.

"To see if I might have brain damage from drinking," she said.

I assured the woman that she did not have brain damage, and I repeated my reassurance on the following day when she requested an electro-encephalogram (brain wave test) to detect brain damage. The next day she wanted a CT scan of the brain. Suspecting that there was something behind this preoccupation with brain damage, I had a lengthy interview with her, and discovered that she was actually hoping that she had brain damage! Why? Because she could then tell her family to stop pressuring her to recover, since she was unable to do so due to brain damage. She would have the ideal excuse why she could neither go to college nor hold a job. As catastrophic as brain damage might be, it would release her from all responsibilities for performance.

The same type of reasoning may prevent a person from recognizing his abilities, because he would then feel obligated to perform at a higher level. A true *cheshbon hanefesh,* a thorough inventory of oneself, is thus essential to discover both the defects which require correction and the strengths which need to be cultivated and implemented.

One should therefore make a detailed list of both one's positive and negative qualities. Attending to the negative column, one should then realize whatever mistakes one has made and resolve not to repeat them. Such a resolve represents a learning experience; i.e., one has learned from one's mistakes not to repeat them. Learning experiences cannot be considered to be negative, and once one has recognized a mistake and resolved not to repeat it, that item should be removed from the negative column and placed in the positive column. A thorough *cheshbon hanefesh* thus performed should facilitate the requisite changes in one's lifestyle.

However, the same factors that contributed to making these mistakes in the first place may also render a person oblivious to their recognition. Furthermore, there may be many blind spots that interfere with recognizing both one's assets and liabilities. The only solution to this is to avail oneself of an objective observer who can pinpoint that which one cannot see himself. This is why the great Chassidic master, Rabbi Elimelich of Lizensk, states in his *Brief Guide to Proper Living* (Paragraph 13):

> One should periodically relate to one's spiritual guide or even to a trusted friend all the thoughts and temptations one had that are forbidden by the Torah which the *yetzer hara* brings to one's mind and heart ... and one should not withhold anything because of shame. By verbalizing them one breaks the strength of the *yetzer hara* ... and one can also

receive valuable advice from the friend. This is a marvelous technique.

Let us listen to what Rabbi Samson Raphael Hirsch says:

> Whatever way a man may take, he thinks it is the right one. He believes it leads to his aim; otherwise he would not follow it. Yet is this goal really the right one? Perhaps the goal itself is outside the direction prescribed by G-d? Perhaps this way which looks so straight to him is in fact a twisting and winding one, leading him astray from the only right direction? All this has to be examined before God and judged according to His Word, for it is God who decides between heart and heart — between the heart whose will is contained in God's will and the heart which subordinates God's will to his own willful one.
>
> And if, after having undergone self-examination, a man absolves himself, he should not trust his own insight without further effort. He should look for advice and instruction at the hand of more understanding people. For: דרך **אויל ישר בעיניו ושמע לעצה חכם** — *The way of an unwise man is straight in his own eyes, but he who listens to advice is wise.* (12:15) ...
>
> ... On the other hand, if a person possesses true wisdom, he will not trust even his own independent judgment too quickly. He will not have unlimited confidence in his own recognition of the right, and will always be afraid of

erring in his own choice. A conceited fool, though, will overstep his limits, for he is either unaware of them or inattentive. He is always confident, and it never occurs to him that he might be mistaken (*From the Wisdom of Mishle,* Feldheim, 1986, pgs. 77,81).

The Torah methodology for making the requisite lifestyle changes thus contains these two vital elements: making a thorough inventory and sharing everything about oneself with another person.

While people may do their utmost to divest themselves of undesirable character traits, there are some which are inherent in a person and which he cannot eradicate. For example, it is possible for a person to avoid going into a rage when provoked, and even to subdue a less intense expression of anger. Incidentally, there is no validity to the frequently quoted idea that if one vents one's anger by screaming or hitting a punching bag, one dissipates it. To the contrary, anger may actually be intensified by such actions. But it is possible to realize that expressing one's anger usually puts others on the defensive, and they fail to hear what one is saying. With a calm demeanor, whereby one delivers the reasons for outrage in a soft tone, one has a far better chance of being heard.

It is also possible to eventually eliminate one's anger by realizing that the offender may have been under a mistaken impression, or that there were extenuating circumstances that caused him to behave in a hostile manner. We can reflect on how often we may have offended someone else and subsequently regretted our actions. Sometimes we have apologized to the person we offended, and sometimes we were too ashamed to apologize, or were afraid of the other person's reaction, or just did not have the opportunity to do so. Whichever, we often wish we had not made the insulting remark or done the injurious act, and we genuinely regret it. Why should we not give the person who offended us the same consideration? Perhaps he too now regrets his behavior.

We may also realize that we stand to gain nothing by bearing a grudge. Torah-observant people know that the Torah not only forbids taking revenge, but that they also may not say, "I will show you that I am a real *mentsch*. I will do you a favor even though you behaved so rudely toward me." Since any acting out of resentments is forbidden, what purpose is there in retaining them? All that may happen is that we will increase the likelihood of getting peptic ulcers, high blood pressure, or migraine headaches. The other person will not be affected by my harboring resentments against him, so why should I punish myself for something someone else did to me? As one person so aptly put it, "Harboring resentments is letting someone you don't like live inside your head rent-free." Why be so magnanimous? Reasoning such as this may enable a person to eventually eliminate the anger one has been harboring.

There is one aspect of anger that cannot be dealt with in this manner, and that is the initial emotion when one is offended or provoked. This appears to be a physiologic reaction that occurs in animals as well as man, and hence is an integral part of our animal nature which we cannot eliminate. However, although *we* cannot eliminate it, it can be eliminated by the One Who put it there. If a person is really bothered by being subject to feelings of anger, he can say to G-d, "Almighty G-d, I really don't like to feel anger. Please remove this feeling from me."

G-d's response may be, "Have you done all you can about this emotion yourself? Have you controlled the expression of anger, which is something well within your ability? Have you rid yourself of resentments, which is something you can do? If you have not done these adequately, go back and do your homework. You are not ready yet to have Me remove this defect. Come back after you have done your homework, and then we can talk."

If you have really done all you can about expressing anger and ridding yourself of resentments, you are then justified in asking G-d to remove the residue. G-d may indeed do so, and many of our *tzaddikim* indeed reached a level of spirituality where they merited Divine removal of anger.

This is very different from the person who *represses* anger, although superficially both may appear identical. Repression of anger may be due to a person feeling he might lose control and act out violently if he were to feel anger, or perhaps he was made to feel so guilty about anger that he would consider himself to be terribly wicked if he felt it. This person, in contrast to the *tzaddik*, actually does feel anger momentarily, but his mind quickly represses it and drives it underground into the subconscious. Its presence in conscious awareness is so fleeting that the person believes that he felt no anger at all.

The trouble with the mechanism of repression is that the anger continues to lurk in the subconscious and constantly tries to push itself into awareness. Much psychological energy is consumed in keeping it buried. Thus, the person who represses anger is constantly engaged in the struggle to keep it in the subconscious. Sometimes the repressed feeling and the pent-up anger may erupt in a violent manner. At other times, it seeks circuitous expression in ways in which it is unrecognizable to the conscious mind, and comes out as passive resistance or severe obstinacy. It is also suspected that repressed anger is a major cause of various physical diseases, notably high blood pressure and migraine headaches.

When G-d removes the anger, however, it is not repressed; it simply does not exist. It is as if He had cut the wires, so that when someone pushes the button that usually would elicit a response of anger, nothing happens. If a person is fortunate enough that G-d has removed the anger, he is then free of the struggle; therefore he does not have to keep it repressed nor deal with it in any other way. The energy that he would have otherwise expended to cope with anger is now free to be directed elsewhere. This is one reason why *tzaddikim* were able to attain such greatness. The energy that we must use to keep certain emotions in check had been released to be used toward greater study of Torah and service of G-d.

It is possible that even if a person has done the necessary homework, G-d may not remove the anger as requested. In His infinite wisdom, He may know that this is not to the person's greatest advantage. There is a certain kind of spirituality that comes only from self-discipline and the exercise of control. Perhaps the person still needs this kind of struggle in spiritual growth, hence his request for Divine removal of anger may be denied.

Just as this is true of anger, it is equally valid for every character trait that a person may wish to eliminate. A person may find himself battling against feelings of greed, envy, hatred, lust, or vanity, and may wish to be free of these. In each case one must become ready to have these defective traits removed, and readiness consists of doing everything within one's power to triumph over them, especially by avoiding the people, places, and things that tend to arouse the undesirable emotions. It is obvious that a person who prays to G-d to relieve him of the struggle with lust, for example, yet who reads immoral material, is nowhere ready for Divine intervention. If, however, a person has done all the homework necessary to put himself in a state of preparedness that justifies Divine intervention, and is indeed fortunate enough to have these defective traits removed, he has taken a giant step toward spirituality.

As we noted earlier, the ethical writings teach that the goal of a person is to achieve a unity with G-d. The

Talmud asks: How is it possible for a person, a finite mortal, to identify with G-d? The Talmud answers: "By emulating the Divine attributes. Just as He is merciful, so should you be merciful. Just as He is forgiving, so should you be forgiving" (*Sotah* 14a). A person who is still in possession of undesirable character traits is far from identifying with G-d, Who is absolute purity, untainted in any way. As the person is freed of these traits, he gradually refines his character and becomes more G-dly. and in this way the ultimate unity with G-d is facilitated. There may be a major barrier to having one's defects removed. The *Shulchan Aruch* says that whereas a person's sins are forgiven on Yom Kippur if he does *teshuvah,* i.e., regrets his misdeeds and resolves not to repeat them, this is inadequate if the sin involved harm to another person. In the latter case, even regret and a sincere resolve not to repeat the act are insufficient (*Orach Chaim* 606). A person must try to rectify the harm that he did to the other person. If he harmed him economically, then he must make restitution. If he insulted him or in any other way offended him, he must apologize and obtain that person's forgiveness. Divine forgiveness cannot be forthcoming until the proper amends to the injured or offended person have been made.

Many people seem to have difficulty in apologizing and asking forgiveness. It is indeed a humbling experience, and the resistance to this seems to be embedded in us from childhood on. Parents will testify how their five-year-old children stubbornly refuse to say, "I'm sorry." The knowledge that one should apologize for having done wrong, together with the discomfort in doing so, result in the human psyche doing one of its clever tricks to spare the person any mental anguish, by making him forget these events. Thus, there may be instances where we offended someone, episodes that we have subsequently put out of our minds. Yet, as noted above, forgiveness is not possible until we do make amends. It may therefore be necessary to exert ourselves to try to recall any instances of having offended someone, so that we can make the necessary amends.

One of the maneuvers our psychological system utilizes as a defense mechanism against our awareness of having done wrong is to rationalize our behavior. We are ingenious in finding reasons whereby we can justify what we have done. This is a grave mistake, and one of the finest rules to live by is, "Never defend a mistake." We are fallible human beings, and it is not a cardinal sin to make a mistake. One of our ethicists points out that on Judgment Day we will be confronted with our sins, and that in our defense, benevolent angels will plead that we were simply too frail to withstand the enormous seductive force of the *yetzer hara*. The prosecuting angels will then argue that even if this is so, why did we not regret our actions after the sin was done, by which time we had satisfied our temptation and were no longer subject to the biological urge to gratify our physical desires? This ethicist points out that whereas committing a sin may be defensible, failure to do *teshuvah* afterward is not defensible.

It is thus common to try to justify our behavior,

and only when all our rationalizations have been proven false do we finally surrender and admit we were wrong. While it is true that it is better late than never, the quality of delayed *teshuvah* is not the noblest, since the person seems to have yielded only with great reluctance and not with full realization of his error.

The Talmud states that whereas King David sinned twice and was forgiven, King Saul sinned only once but was not forgiven. How can this be? When the prophet Samuel reprimanded Saul for disobeying the Divine instructions, Saul protested, "But I did fulfill the will of G-d." Only later, after Samuel's continued rebuke, did Saul admit that he had done wrong, but then it was too late. He had already lost his kingship (*I Samuel* 15:13-25). On the other hand, when the prophet Nathan reprimanded David, he offered no defense whatsoever, but promptly admitted that he had sinned (*II Samuel* 12:1-13). A truly spiritual person will not try to justify a wrong deed.

Some people, who equate spirituality with religion, dichotomize their lives, advocating, "Give onto G-d what is G-d's and give unto Caesar what is Caesar's." They see spirituality as being expressed primarily in prayer and religious rituals. For the Torah-observant person there is no such division. All of one's life must be devoted to the Divine service, and all of one's life must be spiritual. The ethical works state that this is what Solomon meant when he said, "Know Him in all your ways" (*Proverbs* 3:6).

Thus, the principles of spirituality must be applied in all one's affairs.

When one's life is directed toward a spiritual goal, everything that contributes to the maintenance of life and health is elevated to a status of spirituality. Accordingly, since a person cannot function without food and rest, eating and sleeping — which provide one with the energy to pursue spirituality — become spiritual acts themselves. Earning one's livelihood is necessary for survival; hence that too becomes spiritual. Exercising and even judicious entertainment, when done in a manner that contributes to one's optimal function, are as much spiritual acts as are the more obvious spiritual practices.

The lion's share of a person's day is not spent in prayer nor in religious rituals, but rather in work, in transacting business, and in socializing. All these mundane activities can become spiritual acts when performed with sincerity, with honesty, with consideration for others and with intent to reach the ultimate goal. Watching one's speech, not to violate the commandment which forbids *lashon hara,* is highly spiritual, as is keeping one's promises and conducting one's transactions fairly.

The Rabbi of Bobov was once visited by the chief gendarme, who told him of the many responsibilities and duties his position entails. Then, pointing to his police chief's cap, he said, "When I come home from work, I remove my cap, and then I can be at ease, free of my many duties." The Rabbi pointed to his *yarmulke* (skullcap) and said, "When I wear this, I am in the Divine service. Inasmuch as I never remove this, even when I sleep, I am never free of my duties toward G-d." A person can be spiritual twenty-four hours a day.

As we noted at the outset, a person cannot achieve spirituality by his unaided efforts, and prayer for Divine assistance is necessary. In our prayers we ask G-d to remove our character defects. "And purify our hearts to serve You in truth," or "Our merciful Father, have compassion upon us, and put into our hearts the understanding so that we may listen, learn, and observe all the *mitzvos* of the Torah with love. Enlighten us with Your Torah, and make our hearts adhere to Your *mitzvos,* and unify our hearts to love and revere You." And we say, "Cleanse me of my sins and purify me of my faults ... create within me a new heart" (*Psalms* 51:4 ... 12). We thus seek through prayer to rid ourselves of our character defects and strengthen our contact with G-d.

There is one significant prerequisite for our prayers to be accepted, and that is an attitude of sincere humility (*Sotah* 5a). Humility is the basis of all desirable character traits (*Letter of Rambam*). Vanity and arrogance are abominable character traits, so much so, that although G-d does not abandon a sinful person, He does not allow His presence to dwell with someone who is vain and arrogant (*Arachin* 15b). If we wish to approach G-d through prayer, we must therefore humble ourselves before Him.

The more profound one's humility, the more effective his prayer will be. The Talmud (*Taanis* 25b) relates that during a severe drought, Rabbi Eliezer prayed fervently for rain, but his prayers were not heeded, whereas when Rabbi Akiva prayed, his prayers were promptly answered. The commentary *Iyun Yaakov* points out that Rabbi Eliezer was no less a scholar than Rabbi Akiva, but as the latter possessed greater humility, his prayers merited a swift response.

When we achieve a measure of spirituality, we are obligated to share it with others. In Torah there is a concept of *arvus*, of mutual responsibility. There are many people who are caught up in materialistic pursuits or even in frankly self-defeating lifestyles. They may be unaware that they are pursuing a course which cannot yield the happiness they seek. If we have mastered all the above steps and have arrived at a different perspective on life, we should help others achieve the same goal. This does not mean that we knock on people's doors and offer to show them what we have found to be a lifestyle that is truly worthy of G-d's noblest creation. Rather, the serenity and peace of mind that results from leading a truly spiritual life should be so evident that others would be eager to learn our secret, so that they, too, can discard a self-defeating lifestyle and opt for spirituality.

While we tend to be creatures of habit and often plod along day after day without giving serious consideration to an ultimate goal in life, there are moments when we have a brief flash of insight, and we think, "What is this all for? Why am I participating in this rat race?" At these moments we may sense a feeling of emptiness and the futility of our particular lifestyle. We might even briefly resolve to make some kind of change in the way we live. But such insights tend to be like a shooting star — a brief moment of glow, only to disappear completely — and within moments we are back to our usual routine.

These momentary insights are precious, and should not be ignored. The Talmud states that every day a voice emanates from Sinai and declares, "Woe unto people that forsake the Torah" (*Ethics of the Fathers* 6:2). The Baal Shem Tov asked, "Inasmuch as no one has ever heard this voice, of what use is it?" He answered, "Although we cannot hear it as an audible sound, the *neshamah* does hear the voice." The momentary insights that flash through a person's thoughts to arouse him to *teshuvah* occur because his *neshamah* (soul) has heard the heavenly voice. Today, with our knowledge of subliminal stimuli, the Baal Shem Tov's explanation is easily understood. The Divine voice is subliminal, and although we perceive it, we are not aware that we are perceiving it.

A wise person will recognize these precious insights as occasions on which G-d Himself is arousing a person from his slumber, from his habitual rut, and will do something to capture the spiritual awakening so that one does not return to an aimless existence.

One time I wished to arise early in the morning because I needed the extra time to complete a project. I set my alarm clock for an earlier hour, but when it rang, I turned over in bed and shut it off, with the intention of sleeping just a few more moments. I awoke several hours later, having lost the opportunity to work on my project. Several weeks later I had to catch a very early flight and had to arise earlier than usual. Remembering my previous experience and knowing how important it was not to miss that flight, I had to take some measure to avoid shutting off the alarm clock for "just a few more moments" of sleep. I therefore placed the alarm clock at the far corner of the room, where I could not shut it off from the bed. When the alarm rang, I had to get out of bed and go across the room to turn it off, and this enabled me to remain awake and catch the flight.

A cknowledging our nature to forget things, we all make little reminders for ourselves, particularly when the item we wish to remember is important. What I did with the alarm clock was just such a maneuver. I knew from previous experience that I was likely to ignore the awakening and return to sleep, and I took the precaution to avoid this happening.

This is what we must do with a spiritual awakening. G-d is frequently arousing us to turn our lives around, and while we are momentarily aroused out of lethargy, we soon slip back into our routine as though nothing had occurred.

The Chassidic writings tell us to be on the alert for these flashes of insight, and the moment they occur, to capture them and hold onto them. How? By promptly doing some *mitzvah*, because that will help us to retain them. For example, upon feeling such a moment of awareness, we should promptly take a *siddur* or *Tehillim* (*Book of Psalms*) and recite a prayer, or give a few coins to *tzedakah,* or recite the *Shema*, reflecting upon our belief in the unity of G-d, or meditate on *ahavas yisroel* and dedicate ourselves to love one's fellow Jew. Or one may think, "I have *mezuzos* on my doors at home. I am at this very moment fulfilling the *mitzvah* of *mezuzah*." Perhaps this is a good time to resolve to check the *mezuzos* to see that they are intact, something which should be done periodically. One has to be on the alert to seize these precious opportunities and not allow them to go to waste. We are blessed with spiritual awakenings, and it is our responsibility that we do not let our laziness convince us to ignore them and to "turn off the alarm clock and go back to sleep."

From all of the above, we might think that escaping from a self-defeating lifestyle and becoming spiritual must be an extremely complicated process. Moses tells us this is not so. To the contrary, "True observance of Torah does not require one to ascend to Heaven nor to cross the seas, but rather is close to you, in thought, in speech, and in deed" (*Deuteronomy* 30:11-14).

In what way can it be close? First, we must realize what the options are: either to lead a spiritual life or a non-spiritual life. Choosing the latter means that one is abandoning the spirit, that component of man which distinguishes him from animals. A human being without spirituality is essentially a kind of animal, perhaps more intelligent than other animals, but an animal nevertheless. Neglecting the spirit is permitting that unique human feature within oneself to perish. This is why Moses says, "I have placed before you today the life and the good (on the one hand), and the death and the evil (on the other)" (*Deuteronomy* 30:15). Opting to live a non-spiritual life is tantamount to allowing the uniquely human aspect of ourselves to wither away and die.

Every intelligent person who values the dignity of his humanity will choose life, i.e., the spiritual life. In spite of what may seem to be rigorous requirements, living a spiritual life need be neither difficult nor complex.

Incidentally, "difficult" and "complex" are not synonymous. Something can be very difficult, yet very simple. For example, if someone were ordered to lift a very heavy weight, that might be exceedingly difficult, but there is nothing complicated about it. On the other hand, a thorny mathematical problem may be most complicated, yet once a person disentangles the complexity, it may be very easy.

There is nothing complicated about being spiritual. The rules are simple, although one might consider them difficult. Solomon says, "G-d created man simple, and it is man who sought complex calculations" (*Ecclesiastes* 7:29). We can take something as simple as "Don't shout when you are angry," and make it seem very complicated. We can take an instruction such as "Don't pick up the first drink," or "Don't eat sugar," and think about it again and again until we have converted a simple statement into a very complicated one. These complexities, Solomon says, are of our own doing. G-d made man a very straight and uncomplicated creature. All one must do is follow the few simple rules.

But then, one might say, even if uncomplicated, it is very difficult to be spiritual. A person is under constant pressure to react in ways that deter one from spirituality. Temptation constantly surrounds us, whether it be to food, to drink, to lust, to take revenge, to hate, to be envious, or to be greedy. It is most difficult to conduct an entire life of struggle against the forces which lead to non-spiritual behavior.

Moses provided the answer to this as well. "You are standing before G-d *this day* ... to enter a covenant which G-d binds with you *this day*" (*Deuteronomy* 29:9-11). Moses then proceeds to repeatedly stress "this day," to indicate that one need only undertake the struggle for spirituality "this day." It is not too difficult for one to implement the rules of spirituality just this one day.

Yes, but life is not just one day. How is one to continue this struggle for an entire lifetime? The answer is, by taking things one day at a time. There is nothing I can do today about my struggle of tomorrow, so why get involved in something which is unproductive? I can resolve to be spiritual today, and whether I will do so tomorrow is something I can decide on tomorrow. By taking one day at a time, we reduce the challenges to bite-size quantities, so it is now neither complex nor difficult.

The Torah teaches us this insight in the episode of the patriarch Jacob, who had to work for his father-in-law for seven years to gain Rachael's hand in marriage. The Torah tells us that these seven years were as "singular days" because of his great love for her (*Genesis* 29:20). The obvious question is, inasmuch as we know human nature to be just the reverse, that when one is separated from one's beloved, every day seems like an eternity, what sense does it make to say that several years were just as a few days because of his love for her? The answer is that the Torah does not say "a *few* days," but rather *singular* days. In other words, the only way Jacob was able to tolerate the long separation was by surviving one day at a time. Had Jacob looked ahead at the entire seven years of waiting, it might not have been feasible to tolerate, but he took each day one at a time; hence they were "singular" days. He did not worry today how he would tolerate tomorrow's frustration, because tomorrow's stress could be dealt with tomorrow, and there was no point in taking it on today.

Not taking on today what we cannot do anything about today is actually a part of a more comprehensive concept, i.e., not to take on anything that is unchangeable. Save your energies for things that can be changed, but do not obstinately insist on trying to change that which cannot be changed.

Solomon wrote in *Proverbs* (10:27): יראת ה׳ תוסיף ימים ושנות רשעים תקצרנה — *The fear of God prolongs days, while the years of the wicked are too short.*

Rabbi Samson Raphael Hirsch explains: The God-fearing man lives in terms of days, and the law-less one in terms of years; yet even years are not sufficient to bring him the fulfillment of his schemes. The God-fearing man's endeavor, his faith-ful compliance with the Divine commandments, can be successfully accomplished on each and every day. Each day that has been lived through in faithful observance of the Torah is a gain, a profit for him. Having accomplished this, he can have it entered on the life-calendar of his sojourn upon earth; he has not lived in vain. He counts days, not years (see *Psalms* 90, 12).

The lawless person, however, sees the value of his life only in external acquisitions. Such acquisitions, though, come to maturity (reach their full value) under the rays of the earthly sun and need years for their development. Mere days, therefore, are meaningless to the lawless man; he can count only years. But even years are not sufficient to bring him fulfillment of his forever-increasing wishes. This is what our Sages meant when they said: *No man departs from this world having attained half of his desires* (*Koheleth Rabbah* 1, 13). *From The Wisdom Of Mishle,* Feldheim, 1986, pgs 25-26).

The concept of taking one day at a time refers not

only to avoiding the burden of the future but also to relinquishing the burdens of the past. Some people may feel that whereas they may be ready to let go of a self-defeating lifestyle, it is not ready to let go of them. They may feel themselves in the grip of the past.

Torah teaches a unique concept of *teshuvah*. When a person abandons an erroneous past and does so in full sincerity, G-d does what no one else can do. He essentially erases the past. These are the words of the prophet: "I have erased your transgressions like a fog, and your sins like a cloud. Return to Me for I have redeemed you" (*Isaiah* 44:22). Just as when a fog has cleared and a cloud has disappeared there is no trace of their previous existence, so when a person abandons his errant ways in sincere *teshuvah*, his past deeds are erased, leaving no vestige to haunt him.

But do we not find references that indicate that one should always have one's sins before one's eyes (*Psalms* 51:5)? Yes, but these do not mean that a person should forever continue to wallow in guilt. A person should accept Divine forgiveness. What these references mean is that a person should recognize his vulnerability. If I have committed a particular sin, I must be aware that this happened because I had the susceptibility of yielding to a particular temptation, and that I must therefore have a heightened state of alertness in that particular area.

A person with thirty years of sobriety recalled how he had been hospitalized after a heavy drinking binge, and how he had suffered severe withdrawal symptoms. "I can remember the terrifying hallucinations, being tied to the bed with leather straps, struggling to escape from the frightening monstrosities that were threatening me, my back in mortal pain from convulsions, clawing with my fingernails at the restraints, until my fingers bled. I remember this so well, and *may I never forget it.*" This man wishes to remember the horror of that experience so that he would be discouraged from repeating the behavior that could lead to its recurrence.

With proper *teshuvah*, our sins are indeed forgiven, totally eradicated. While we should accept the forgiveness and feel completely cleansed and no longer need to carry any *guilt* for our transgression, we should retain the memory of it so that the realization of the gravity of its effects on our spirituality will deter us from repeating the particular behavior.

Relinquishing the past and adopting a new way of life essentially gives rise to a new person, a new entity, as Rambam states, "I am no longer the person that sinned" (*Hil. Teshuvah* 2:4).

Rambam states that proper *teshuvah* is achieved when G-d will testify that this person will never again repeat the sinful act (*ibid* 2:2). This statement elicited a question from many commentaries, that inasmuch as the Divine foreknowledge does not determine a person's behavior, and a person always has complete freedom to choose to do either right or wrong, how can G-d testify that someone will never again do a particular sin? This appears to contradict the principle of total free will.

I was provided with the answer to this by a man who delivered a talk on the twenty-fifth anniversary of his sobriety. He said, "The man I once was drank, and the man I once was will drink again. I am sober today because I am not the same person who drank. If I ever go back to being that person, I will drink again."

What Rambam is saying is that sins do not occur in a vacuum. A person who rises in the early hours of the morning to study Torah, and then attends the morning service, does not wrap up his *tefillin* and hurry to a *treifah* restaurant for breakfast. A sin occurs only when a person is in a weakened state of spirituality which allows him to commit that sin. Hence it is not sufficient for a person to be remorseful over a sin, but he must also analyze, "How did it ever happen that I could do that?" He must then rid himself of those character defects that made that sin possible, and he must reach a new state of spirituality. In this new state of spirituality he cannot commit that sin.

Rambam says that adequate *teshuvah* requires reaching a new state of spirituality, and since only G-d knows when this has occurred, *teshuvah* is only complete when G-d testifies that the person has indeed reached this new state, and *as long as he does not descend from that level of spirituality* he will not commit that sin again.

The contradiction of Divine testimony and free will is now resolved. It is, of course, possible that a person may not maintain the level of spirituality he had reached, and if he drops from that level of spirituality, he is prone to sin again. G-d does not testify that he will never sin again, but that the level of spirituality he has now reached through *teshuvah* is one which will not allow that sin to occur.

The concept of one day at a time allows a person to be truly free, free of the unnecessary worries of the future, and free from the burden of the past. This freedom allows one to adopt a new lifestyle.

The Talmud states that if a man prays that his pregnant wife should have a boy, it is a futile prayer (*Berachos* 54a). The child is already male or female, and it is absurd to pray for a miraculous change. True, G-d can do anything, and has performed many miracles that have transcended the laws of nature, yet to ask G-d to alter reality is considered a prayer of futility. One must learn to accept reality and to put one's efforts into making those changes that are within the realm of actuality. But how is one to know whether what one desires is changeable or not? Sometimes we may so intensely desire something that we may refuse to accept its being impossible. The answer is that for this, too, we must pray, i.e., for G-d to give us the insight and wisdom so that we may be able to distinguish that which is changeable from that which is not.

Another basic component of spirituality is *gratitude*, whose overwhelming importance should be evident from the fact that upon arising in the morning, the very first words a person should say are *modeh ani*, I thank You, G-d. Our prayers are replete with expressions of thanks to G-d for everything He has done for us.

Some people seem to have a great deal of difficulty with gratitude. It seems as though being aware of gratitude towards someone imposes an obligation toward one's benefactor, and since they do not wish to be beholden to anyone, they simply deny that they have any reason to feel grateful. A spiritual person is not frightened by feelings of gratitude. One should be able to accept a favor graciously, and although one need not feel obligated nor beholden to a benefactor, there is really nothing wrong with returning a kindness.

Truthfulness is the basis of all spirituality, and rigorous honesty is the *sine qua non* for recovery from all self-defeating lifestyles. The alcoholic notoriously lies about his drinking, the compulsive eater about food, and the gambler about gambling. A person whose goal is accumulation of more wealth will lie to acquire more money, and someone who is in pursuit of honor and fame will lie to acquire acclaim.

Torah places great importance on truthfulness. Indeed, one of the ethicists states that the *yetzer hara* is ready to relinquish a person from all other temptations in return for falsehood, because if a person deviates from the truth, this will eventually result in the self-destruction which is the aim of the *yetzer hara*.

The reason for the primacy of truth should be evident. The truth of man's existence and his purpose in the universe is that he seek closeness with G-d. Anyone who pursues truth will therefore find his way to G-d, because that is where the truth is found. We complete the reading of the *Shema* with the words

"G-d is truth." Pursuit of truth is thus equivalent to reaching out to G-d. With truth there is everything, and without truth there is nothing.

Torah is most demanding and uncompromising on truth. Truth is like a hermetically sealed container, where even a pinhole opening destroys the entire seal. Neither "white lies" nor any other variety are condoned. Ethicists say that the oft-quoted aphorism attributed to the Talmud that one may lie in order to restore peace and harmony between man and wife or among friends is in itself a lie, because the Talmud never stated this. It is a principle of Torah that the end does not justify the means, and that committing a sin for a noble purpose is not permissible; hence it is forbidden to lie even for the lofty purpose of restoring peace and harmony. A careful reading of the Talmud teaches that in order to restore peace a person may present things in such a manner that the parties involved will each draw the conclusion that the other party regrets being at odds and wishes to reconcile. One may therefore word matters in such a way that the listener may interpret this in a manner which would lead to abandoning hostilities, and even this is permissible only for the restoration of peace and harmony, but not for any other purpose. Aside from very few specific and well-defined instances, frank lying is never permitted.

Another reason for the pivotal role of rigorous honesty is that it influences a person's behavior. In addition to the Scriptural prohibition against lying (*Leviticus* 19:11), the Torah also states, "Keep a distance from falsehood" (*Exodus* 23:7). What is meant by "keeping a distance from falsehood"?

A person may do something which essentially sets the stage for lying. If there is ever a need that he may have to deny his action, then his doing that particular deed is setting the stage for lying in the future. Keeping one's distance from lying therefore means that a person should avoid doing anything which he might subsequently have to deny. Just a bit of introspection will reveal that if a person is so committed to truth that he will refrain from doing anything that might necessitate lying, his behavior will be impeccable, and his life will be highly spiritual.

The effort to overcome a self-destructive lifestyle is both enhanced and facilitated when it is done with a group rather than by oneself. Indeed, when a person tries to make a major change in himself without some kind of external help, it is often doomed to failure. It is clearly stated in the Talmud that a scholar who learns Torah alone, not sharing his study with a companion, may actually become less learned rather than wiser (*Makkos* 10a).

Experience has proven the validity of this, because when learning in solitude, one may make a wrong interpretation and arrive at an erroneous conclusion, and then proceed on that basis, thereby distorting everything he subsequently learns. Even if he is later set straight, the harm of having learned something incorrectly may not be easily undone. "Once a mistake becomes ingrained, it tends to remain" (*Pesachim* 112a). Learning in a group minimizes this source of error, since it is likely that someone will note and alert one to a mistake. The Talmud states that the larger the group that learns Torah together, the more meritorious it is (*Berachos* 6a).

This is true of prayer as well as of the study of Torah. Although it is permissible for a person to pray individually, *halachah* places great emphasis on the virtue of *tefillah betzibur*, praying together as a group. The Talmud states that the prayer of an assembly is more favorably received (*ibid.* 8a). We have noted how important prayer is in invoking Divine assistance to know G-d's will and to remove character defects, and people praying together for this purpose reinforce one another's prayers. In addition, by associating with others, one can benefit greatly from the experience of those who can enlighten one with helpful techniques that have proven effective, and with means to avoid pitfalls in self-improvement.

Our ethicists cite the verse in *Genesis*, "Jacob remained alone, and a man wrestled with him" (32:25). The Midrash states that this attacker was the patron angel of Esau, who sought to destroy Jacob spiritually if not physically, but could only attempt this when Jacob was alone.

The Torah states that Israel will be so strong that "five of you will pursue one hundred of your enemies, and one hundred of you will pursue ten thousand" (*Leviticus* 26:8). Rashi notes that these figures are not mathematically correct, because if five pursue one hundred, the ratio is then that one hundred will pursue *two* thousand, rather than ten thousand. Rashi answers that there is strength in numbers, and that the relationship is exponential rather than linear. Five may subdue one hundred, but one hundred people working together can triumph over ten thousand. Individuals involved in altering a self-destructive lifestyle should therefore seek each other out and work together toward their common goal.

There is yet another advantage to working within a group. The Baal Shem Tov said that inasmuch as most people are oblivious to their own character defects (clearly the Baal Shem Tov understood *denial* very well), G-d provides them with an opportunity to become aware of these. The world, said the Baal Shem Tov, is like a mirror, in that the defects that you perceive in others are actually your own. Sharing oneself with others thus provides a valuable opportunity to discover defects in oneself that might otherwise go unnoticed.

By the same token, we have noted that some people are unable to see their own personality strengths, and focus only on their negative features. Here, too, the group experience can be invaluable.

When a person sees how others are oblivious to their own character assets, it may set him to thinking, "Perhaps I, too, am unaware of the notable aspects of my personality." The group experience thus facilitates achieving a thorough self-awareness.

It is absolutely vital to establish proper priorities, and failure to do so can have grave consequences. One physician who began his recovery from alcoholism told me that he was attending three AA meetings daily. When I asked him how he was able to fit these meetings into his practice of medicine, he said, "I don't fit my meetings into my practice; rather, I fit my practice into the meetings. If I don't attend three meetings daily, I will not have a practice." He is now sober some twenty years, and while at present he attends three meetings a week instead of a day, his attitude of giving his sobriety top priority has prevailed.

When Rabbi Yisroel of Salant championed the cause of formal study of *mussar* (ethics), someone asked him, "I can only set aside fifteen minutes a day for Torah study. Should I spend this on study of *mussar* or Talmud?"

"*Mussar*, of course," Rabbi Yisroel said.

"Do you mean to say that *mussar* is more important than Talmud?" the man challenged.

"Not at all," said Rabbi Yisroel, "but if you will study *mussar* for fifteen minutes, you will become aware that you can find three hours for study of Talmud."

Priority must be given to eliminating self-defeating behavior. First things first. All the material wealth in the world and all the knowledge one can accumulate are of no value whatever if a person destroys himself.

The Talmud and the ethical works refer to the *yetzer hara* as the eternal enemy, which constantly seeks to destroy a person. "The *yetzer hara*, Satan, and the angel of death, are one and the same" (*Bava Basra* 16a). The *yetzer hara* is relentless, and it never retreats from its efforts to destroy a person; hence one must eternally be on guard. The ways of this enemy are many, and the *yetzer hara* is described as being cunning, baffling, and powerful. Whether the destructive force takes the shape of compulsive eating, drinking, gambling, smoking, or any of the other self-defeating behaviors that are either spiritually or physically injurious, it is all the same. The cunning of the *yetzer hara* is often evident when it causes a person to delude himself that he has improved, whereas what has actually happened is that he really substituted one self-defeating behavior for another.

W e have just completed a series of essential steps for reversing a self-defeating lifestyle, whatever its particular manifestations may be. All of these steps have been drawn from the Talmud and the writings of *mussar*. I have compiled these primarily at the request of those who felt that obeying Torah should obviate the need for a Twelve Step recovery program, but anyone familiar with the Twelve Step program will recognize the strong similarity between the two.

For those who may not be familiar with the Twelve Steps of recovery, let me cite them to you. These happen to refer to alcoholism, but one can substitute the word "drugs," "food," "gambling," "anger," "procrastination," or any other self-defeating condition for the word "alcohol."

Step One

We admitted we were powerless over alcohol — that our lives had become unmanageable.

Step Two

Came to believe that a Power greater than ourselves could restore us to sanity.

Step Three

Made a decision to turn our will and our lives over to the care of G-d as we understood Him.

Step Four

Made a searching and fearless moral inventory of ourselves.

Step Five

Admitted to G-d, to ourselves, and to another human being the exact nature of our wrongs.

Step Six

Were entirely ready to have G-d remove all these defects of character.

Step Seven

Humbly asked Him to remove our shortcomings.

Step Eight

Made a list of all persons we had harmed, and became willing to make amends to them all.

Step Nine

Made direct amends to such people wherever possible, except when to do so would injure them or others.

Step Ten

Continued to take personal inventory and when we were wrong promptly admitted it.

Step Eleven

Sought through prayer and meditation to improve our conscious contact with G-d as we understood Him, praying only for knowledge of His will for us and the power to carry that out.

Step Twelve

Having had a spiritual awakening as the result of these steps, we tried to carry this message to alcoholics, and to practice these principles in all our affairs.

It is difficult to see where these are incompatible with Torah.

Why, then, do some people shun Twelve Step programs, claiming that they prefer a Torah approach instead? One reason may be because the preponderance of meetings held in church basements have led to the impression that the Twelve Step programs are

Christian programs, and since Jews are and have always been wary of missionary movements, they suspect the Twelve Step programs as being proselytizing. The simple fact is that the meetings were held almost exclusively in churches because synagogues did not make themselves available. The traditional belief that *"shikker iz a goy"* resulted in rabbis and community officials assuming that there was no reason for such meetings to be held in Jewish facilities. When Overeaters Anonymous came along, a program highly desirable for a population that grew up hearing *"ess, ess, mein ziss kind"* (eat, eat, my sweet child), the identification with churches that characterized Alcoholics Anonymous carried over to Overeaters Anonymous, along with the suspicion that it is an evangelistic movement.

At Twelve Step meetings, one may hear many concepts which are found in the Torah. For example, one recovering woman described the anger and bitterness she felt when she lost her job and when her marriage broke up. She was angry at G-d, protesting, "Why are You doing this to me?"

"But now," she said, "after several years of sobriety, I can see that G-d was right and I was wrong. That marriage was a sick marriage, and I am now developing a healthy relationship. I am soon to receive my master's degree, which I could never have gotten had I remained in that job. I can now see that G-d took away from me those things that I did not have sense enough to give up by myself."

This is clearly a Torah concept, as the Talmud tells

us about the greatness of Nahum ish Gamzu, who accepted everything that happened as benevolent, even things that were very distressing. Also, the Talmud tells us that a person should be grateful to G-d for everything, the bad that occurs as well as the good (*Berachos* 54a). Just as an infant who is being immunized by a painful injection cannot understand why his mother allows the doctor to inflict pain on him, so we are often unable to understand why a benevolent G-d allows us to experience suffering.

One recovering person said, "For a long time I was so obtuse that I could not recognize the pattern, but I have now come to realize that when something bad happens, it is always a prelude to something good. So now, when something bad happens, I become excited with the curiosity and anticipation of what is the good that is certain to follow."

One may hear a recovering person say, "I have found that there are no coincidences. Coincidences are actually miracles in which G-d prefers to remain anonymous." What a wonderful way to express the concept of *hashgachah*, Divine providence! We may think that some things "just happen," but there are no "just happenings." With the exception of moral free choice which G-d has delegated to man, G-d operates everything in the world.

At a "gratitude" meeting where most of the attendants expressed thankfulness for the favorable turn in their lives, one recovering person said, "I have been sober for four years, and I wish I could tell you that it has all been good. Last year my plant closed down and I have been out of work. My wife is suing for divorce. I fell behind in my mortgage payments and the bank foreclosed on my home. My car has been repossessed. But I know that G-d did not bring me all this way just to walk out on me now."

In the Shabbos prayer of *Nishmas* we say, "You have saved us from the sword, and spared us from the plague, and You have raised us above terrible diseases. Your mercies have been with us until this time, and Your kindness has not deserted us, and You will *never* abandon us unto eternity." We have often said the words, but have we said them with conviction?

The Baal Shem Tov said that we had no concept of how intensely G-d loves us. "I wish I could love the greatest *tzaddik* as much as G-d loves the worst *rasha* (sinful person)." The wife of a recovering addict, who is herself involved in a recovery program, related how she was initially devastated when, after a long struggle with infertility, she finally conceived and had her longed-for child, who was born with Down's Syndrome. The recovery program helped her accept the Divine wisdom, and she said, "When I realize how deeply I love that little child in spite of his defects, then I can understand how G-d can love me even with all my defects."

One woman said, "I am grateful to be at this meeting tonight. It is the first time in three months that I have left my home since undergoing surgery for removal of a cancerous kidney. What this program has done for me is to help me accept my life as it is rather than as I would like it to be."

A physician who suffered a heart attack during his drinking years said, "I lay there in the intensive care unit, hooked up to all kinds of contraptions, weak and helpless. I was angry at G-d for doing this to me. I did not realize that G-d had seized me by the shoulders and shaken me, trying to get me to see that I needed to change the way I was living. It was not until much later, in retrospect, that I was able to appreciate His intervention."

A highly successful attorney confided, "When I was forty, I had achieved more than I had ever dreamt of. I was making loads of money, I had a beautiful family, luxurious home, and held prestigious positions in my profession and in the community. I did not realize that my personal life was a shambles due to my drinking, and when my family confronted me, I thought they were crazy. In order to avoid the breakup of my family, I reluctantly consented to treatment, and only after this did I discover why I drank. I had everything, yet I had nothing. There was virtually nothing I lacked for, yet my life was empty."

In the book *Twelve Steps and Twelve Traditions* (AA World Services, Inc., 1973) we read, "In all these strivings, so many of them well-intentioned, our crippling handicap had been our lack of humility. We had lacked the perspective to see that character-building and spiritual values had to come first, and that material satisfactions were not the purpose of living. Quite characteristically, we had gone all out in confusing the ends with the means. Instead of regarding the satisfaction of our material desires as the means by which we could live and function as human beings, we had taken these satisfactions to be the final end and aim of life."

All these concepts appear to be so "Torah-dik." How did people who are not familiar with Torah arrive at these? The answer is quite simple. The Talmud states that if the Torah had not been given, people would have been obligated to derive rules of proper conduct from observation of nature. For example, they would have learned respect for private property by observing ants, because if an ant has procured a piece of grain, no other ant will touch it. They would have learned fidelity from observing doves, who are monogamous, and so on (*Eruvin* 100a). But one may ask, without the Torah as a guide, who is to say that man would have made the proper observations? Perhaps he would have learned rapaciousness from tigers and promiscuity from dogs.

As we noted earlier, *Ecclesiastes* says that "G-d created man straight and simple, but man sought to complicate things with his calculations" (72:9). Man's pristine nature would have led him to make the correct observations to learn proper moral behavior. If man does not do so, it is because he is deterred by his temptations to justify the kind of behavior that would gratify his physical desires.

A person who has led a self-defeating lifestyle and has come to the painful realization that behavior motivated by self-gratification is self-destructive, and is ready to make a change which will give his life substance and meaning, is in a position to avoid the lure of temptation. His experience has proven to him that such behavior is devastating. If he is ready to set aside the search for gratification and is ready to embark on a search for truth, he will find the principles of proper living in the correct observation of nature and of the universe, as the Talmud points out.

One might say, "Fine, then. If I follow the principles of a recovery program, I have no need for Torah observance, right?"

Wrong, very wrong. The recovery program requires turning one's life over to the will of G-d. How can we possibly know what is the will of G-d without Torah? For the Jew, the observance of Torah, both the Scriptures and the Oral Law, are the will of G-d. For the non-Jew, the seven categories of the Noahite *mitzvos* are the will of G-d.

The Talmud ascribes to G-d the words, "I created the *yetzer hara*, and I created Torah as its antidote" (*Kiddushin* 30b). The *yetzer hara* bombards us day in and day out, twenty-four hours a day, with temptations that detract from spirituality. The only effective technique whereby the *yetzer hara's* machinations can be thwarted and whereby spirituality can be achieved is the observance of the Torah and *mitzvos*.

As we previously noted, anyone acquiring a highly complex appliance or piece of machinery will carefully read the manufacturer's instructions for proper operation. Failure to do so and trying to operate the apparatus according to one's own understanding may result not only in inefficient function, but can also cause irreparable damage.

The Torah is the "Manufacturer's instruction manual," provided for us by the Creator. If a person tries to operate this multi-system organism without following the Manufacturer's instructions, the organism is likely to malfunction, and he may cause it to sustain severe damage. For these reasons, full Torah observance is essential to avoid self-defeating behavior and to achieve the spiritual life which dignifies human existence.

Some people have asked, inasmuch as the Twelve Step recovery program has proven to be so effective in the treatment of chemical dependencies, why is it not applied as a preventive technique? Why do we not institute teaching of the Twelve Steps in elementary schools, so that youngsters will not take to alcohol or drugs?

The answer is that living the Twelve Step program requires rigorous self-discipline and involves denying oneself many of the pleasures people desire. A true commitment of turning one's life over to the will of G-d, of "making His will your will" may restrict a person from pursuing various physical indulgences which cannot be seen as being within the Divine will. It is rather unrealistic to expect a person who is living within the Western civilization's ethos of pleasure seeking to deny himself these pleasures.

The person who has led a life of self-defeating behavior may reach a point where he simply cannot continue that lifestyle. The consequences have simply become too distressful, and he realizes that he must institute a change in order to survive. This is what is often referred to as having reached "rock bottom."

Another reason why prevention is not feasible in a secular world is due to the absence of an ultimate goal. Several years ago, a campaign of "Just Say No To Drugs" was launched to discourage young people from drug usage. Psychologists who asked youngsters for their reaction to this slogan were taken aback when several young people aged thirteen or fourteen reacted, "Why? What else is there?"

It is understood that there are objectives for which a person should make sacrifices. The concept of *mesiras nefesh* is based on the conviction that the quest for the ultimate goal is what gives life its meaning and value, and if a person is in a situation where that goal is in jeopardy, he must choose to yield his very life rather than betray that goal. In lesser degrees, we all make sacrifices for whatever we consider to be important goals.

In a secular culture where the ultimate goal of life has become pleasure seeking, there is no adequate justification for asking young people to make any sacrifice and deny themselves the pleasure of chemicals in favor of an ultimate goal, since that goal itself is none other than the selfsame pleasure. Young people tend to believe that they are immune to the dangers of drugs, and if there is no other viable ultimate goal to make life worth living, they will pursue the accepted cultural goal of seeking immediate pleasure wherever and whenever they can get it, irrespective of the risks involved or the penalty exacted.

By definition, prevention is intended for those

people who have not yet adopted a self-defeating lifestyle, in the hope that they can be deterred from doing so. Since they have in no way reached "rock bottom" nor suffered any negative consequences, it is most unlikely that they will adopt a lifestyle that will deny them various pleasures.

Torah education should overcome this obstacle. A child reared in a truly Torah-observant home and educated in a Torah manner should be able to adopt the Torah principles of living even without having reached "rock bottom." Torah education also emphasizes the ultimate goal of achieving a closeness with G-d by developing oneself spiritually. A Torah lifestyle should thus be the ideal preventive program for avoidance of self-defeating behaviors. It can indeed do so, provided that it is adopted fully, with total adherence to both *halachah and mussar*. Failure to live up to all the ethical requirements of Torah will undo its effectiveness.

There is an important similarity between the Torah approach to behavior and the Twelve Step program approach. and both differ with the traditional psychotherapeutic approach. For many years, psychologists had assumed that understanding is essential to behavior, both from cognitive and therapeutic aspects. The theory behind traditional psychotherapy was that the patient should be helped to understand the origins of his behavior, on the assumption that if a person understood the dynamics underlying his behavior, he could easily change it. This approach proved so routinely unsuccessful in addictive conditions, and people who underwent dynamic psychotherapy kept on drinking for years while trying with their therapist to figure out just why they are drinking.

The Twelve Step program took a different approach. "Don't pick up the first drink, and go to meetings." The sequence of events was to first stop the self-defeating behavior, and subsequently one may try to understand its causes. It is an accepted observation in alcoholism that if you try to reason why you should not drink, you will end up drinking. The same holds true for various self-defeating behaviors.

In the Torah we find a similar approach. One does not enter into a discussion or argument with the *yetzer hara*. Whatever reasons you can propose for one position, the *yetzer hara* will give several logical reasons to the contrary. The Talmud states that there was a clever scholar who could give one hundred and fifty logical arguments why a rodent should be considered a ritually pure animal, while the simple fact is that the Torah designates it as ritually impure. The principle of "control behavior first and do your calculations later" is contained in the episode of Joseph, who resisted the temptation of the wife of Potiphar. The Torah states that at the onset he refused, and after that he gave his reasons why (*Genesis* 39:8). The commentaries state that this is how Joseph was able to resist the temptation, but had he tried to argue his position in order to arrive at a conclusion about his behavior, he might well have succumbed to the temptation. A successful attorney with many years of sobriety related how he was initially unsuccessful in remaining sober even though he was attending AA meetings regularly. He asked one of the senior members, "What is it that I am doing wrong?"

"I've been watching you, son," the veteran said. "I'll tell you what you're doing wrong. You're trying to figure out how and why this program works. That will get you drunk. Just do as you're told, don't try to figure out why."

The attorney related, "That was the most demeaning and insulting remark I had ever heard. I am not an imbecile. I am a highly intelligent person and I am a lawyer. I don't do things unless I understand why."

"Later that night," the attorney continued, "I got to thinking that my way of trying to understand had not been successful, whereas that old-timer must be doing something right, because he is still sober. Even though it was an anathema to me, I decided I would give his way a try for just a short period. That short period has now extended itself to thirty-two years of sobriety."

When the Israelites received the Torah, they accepted it with the declaration of "We will do and we will listen (understand)." The principle is clearly stated here: First do as you are instructed, whether or not you understand why. After you have done what you are told, you may try to fathom why.

The Talmud provides a formula for preventing self-destructive practices. First, it gives the basis for self-defeating behavior: "Envy, physical desires, and pursuit of acclaim drive a person out of the world" (*Ethics of the Fathers* 4:21). The common denominator of these three traits is that they are bottomless pits, and they can literally take a person out of the world. A person who is envious of others is never satisfied with what he has, even if he has more than others. It is a fact of nature that physical desires have no endpoint, and people who crave recognition are forever desirous of more and greater honors. Eliminating these three traits would prevent much of the frustration and discontent that fuels self-defeating behavior.

The Talmud also provides the antidotes to them. "The world is based on three things; Torah, service of G-d, and acts of benevolence" (*ibid.* 1:2). Just as the three traits listed above take a person out of the world, these three things maintain him within the world. Rambam states that physical passions occur only in a heart that is devoid of Torah (*Hil. Isurei Biah* 22:21). In the same vein, the Rabbi of Kotzk said that one should not sin not only because it is forbidden, but because one should not have free time to sin. If one is occupied pursuing those activities one should be doing in observance of Torah, there simply would not be an opportunity to sin.

A person who is sincerely devoted to the service of G-d cannot be vain. One who clearly recognizes the Majesty of G-d and who effaces himself in the Divine presence cannot pursue ego aggrandizement. And finally, acts of benevolence, giving of oneself to others, whether by sharing one's possessions or by devoting one's efforts to others, constitute the antidote for envy.

Proper observance of Torah, not only by comply-
ing with the ritual requirements but also by adopting
all the spiritual principles of Torah, can be highly
effective in preventing self-defeating behaviors.

A lcoholics Anonymous has a slogan: "Let go and Let G-d." This is an important principle, but it must be properly understood within the guidelines of Torah teachings.

Our ethical works discuss the concepts of *bitachon*, trust in G-d, and *hishtadlus*, making an effort to get our objectives accomplished. The essence of the issue is this. A person is required to take proper action to achieve things in a natural manner, and must pray for the Divine blessing that his efforts turn out well. For example, it is required that a sick person seek competent medical treatment, and pray to G-d for recovery. Similarly, a person is required to do something constructive to earn a living, and to pray to G-d that his efforts be blessed with success. This perspective is based on the Scriptural verse "G-d will bless you in all the work that you do" (*Deuteronomy* 15:18); i.e., a person must *do*, but must realize that it is the Divine blessing that will bring his efforts to fruition.

We have mentioned that workaholism is one of the self-defeating behaviors. The Talmud states that the amount of money a person will earn is predetermined on Rosh Hashanah (*Beitzah* 16b) and one cannot exceed this fixed amount by exerting oneself, however strenuously. A person should therefore engage in work or in business, but should realize that he must limit his time in these ventures, and devote adequate time to prayer, the study of Torah, and performance of *mitzvos*. One should also allow for quality time with one's family. Come to think of it, no one has ever said in the last days of life, "My only regret is that I did not spend more time at the office." Since one will ultimately regret not having spent more time in spiritual pursuits, why not do it now and avoid the need for regret?

According to the Midrash, man was initially created to be able to devote his entire life to spirituality. It was only after he sinned that it was decreed, "By the sweat of your brow will you eat your bread" (*Genesis* 3:19).

The necessity to work for a living was thus instituted as a punishment. What reasonable person would seek to increase his own punishment? Logic dictates that one should do only as much as necessary, and rely on the Divine blessing for all that he needs.

The concept of "Let go and let G-d" means precisely that a person should do that which is within his realm to do, and whatever is beyond that realm should be left to G-d. Since the amount a person will ultimately earn is Divinely dictated, it is therefore not within one's sphere to increase one's total earnings. Accepting this principle would relieve a person from the bondage of workaholism.

There are other applications of the "Let go and let G-d" principle. A while back I received a very aggravating telephone call from a woman I did not know, and although I tried to contain my frustration, I eventually did use some very sharp and critical words. I subsequently regretted having been so caustic, even though my position was more than justified. I wished to apologize to the woman for the way I had spoken, but unfortunately, not knowing her identity, I was unable to apologize, and I was very upset by this.

On the following day I happened to attend an AA meeting at which people brought up topics they wished to discuss. I mentioned how badly I was feeling for I had been offensive to someone and could not apologize for it.

One of the people at the meeting asked, "And just what do you intend to accomplish by carrying that guilt? It will not make that woman feel any better, and will only eat away at you. If you wish to apologize to her but are unable to do so, then it is out of your hands. Turn it over to your Higher Power. Let go and let G-d."

Just a few days later, I read in a volume on *mussar* that if a person has harmed or offended someone, and sincerely wishes to make amends but is unable to locate that person, he should be secure that G-d will instill within that person the idea to forgive him. In this way the condition essential for achieving absolution by receiving the forgiveness of the person one had offended can be satisfied. When one can no longer do anything about a certain situation, one must "Let go." The person who has *emunah* (faith) will realize that when one has let go, G-d takes over.

Because self-defeating behaviors have been habitual to a person, there is always the possibility that even after a person has altered his lifestyle, he may regress to his self-defeating behavior, particularly when he is stressed. Caution needs to be taken to avoid such relapses, yet if a relapse should occur, it should not be considered a catastrophe. Rather, one should reevaluate one's recovery program and try to find out where one may have been lax, and what new methods might be necessary to deal with the present situation. Although a relapse is unfortunate, it can be converted into a stimulus for new growth and progress in spirituality. In fact, while it is certainly best avoided, the growth subsequent to relapse may not be achievable in any other way.

This concept is found in *mussar*. Rabbi Chaim

Shmulevitz cites the Talmudic comment on the verse in *Michah* 7:8 that growth spurts may sometimes be preceded by a fall in spirituality. Rabbi Shmulevitz states that it is possible for an individual to rise to a level of spirituality and remain fixated at that level without progressing further, so that although he is now functioning at a higher level of spirituality than previously, his behavior has become routine and habitual. Even *mitzvos*, if performed without enthusiasm and as a matter of rote, lose much of their value, and the only thing that may shake a person out of his routine is some kind of trauma in the form of a significant drop in spirituality. While such a descent is undesirable, it may serve the purpose of arousing the person out of the lethargy of habit and introducing new vigor into his spirituality (5732:37).

You may have noted a car bearing a bumper sticker saying "Easy does it." This invariably means that the driver belongs to a Twelve Step program, and has been urged to develop a calm demeanor, not only for ethical reasons, but because getting all worked up and shouting is generally counterproductive. When you lose your composure and scream, you are likely to put people on the defensive, and then they fail to hear what you are saying.

The *mussar* writings frequently cite the verse in *Ecclesiastes* (9:17), "The words of the wise are listened to when they are said calmly." Keeping one's composure is not only virtuous, but simply more practical and productive.

I believe I have demonstrated what the necessary components of a recovery program are. I can also assure you that there is a significant incidence of many types of self-defeating behavior among Jews and even among Jews who practice varying degrees of Torah observance. These people are suffering personally, inflicting much damage upon themselves, and are also placing much emotional stress on those about them, and causing significant harm to those who are dearest to them. It is unconscionable that such misery be permitted to continue when there is relief available. I can empathize with the cry of the prophet, "Why do you continue to be smitten and yet persist in deviating" (*Isaiah* 1:5)?

If there are those who, for whatever reason, do not wish to affiliate with any of the existing recovery programs, my suggestion is, "Why not devise a recovery program of your own?" After all, Alcoholics Anonymous was initiated in 1935 by only two people. Let two or more people join together to launch a recovery program that embodies the necessary components. Let them call themselves whatever name they wish, and let them meet in the privacy of their homes or in synagogues.

But let me point out, we know that the AA model works. If you wish to develop a similar program, I strongly urge that you do not deviate from the model that has proven itself successful. Some people who have tried to tailor a recovery program to their own needs and whims have omitted crucial elements, resulting in an ineffective program. In our daily prayers we cite the Talmudic description of the preparation of incense in the Temple service, and after all the ingredients are listed, the Talmud states that one dare not add honey to the mixture, and that if one omits even a single ingredient, he has committed a capital offense (*Kereisos* 6a). Similarly, if one tries to "sweeten" the recovery program, or omit any of its essential ingredients, it will cause a fatal flaw.

A recovery program cannot belong to any group or

sect. It cannot have a president or guru, hence there is no room for personal ambition, and not only can it not be profit making, but it must also be entirely self-supporting, declining any outside contributions. It cannot affiliate with any organization, religious or secular. It does not offer opinions on any outside issues, hence it does not get involved in any public controversy. A recovery program is interested in only one thing: providing for the recovery of its members. A group formed according to these principles and abiding by them, and incorporating all of the Talmudic and *mussar* teachings cited, will be a very effective recovery group regardless of whatever its name may be.

Perhaps the rabbi can serve as a catalyst for the formation of such groups. The rabbi may set the stage for the development of such alliances by speaking about these issues from the pulpit, and addressing them in the congregation's newsletter. He may then put a notice on the bulletin board and in the congregation's bulletin to the effect that parties interested in the formation of self-help groups for addressing self-defeating behaviors such as alcoholism, chemical dependency, compulsive gambling, eating disorders, rage-aholism, or workaholism may call the rabbi, and stress that confidentiality will be guaranteed. Although there will not be a stampede, there will likely be some people who will respond, and with their mutual consent, they can be brought together to form the nucleus of a group.

But why are such groups essential? Since the principles are all of Talmudic and *mussar* origin, why not just have the rabbi offer more *shiurim* (classes) on these subjects?

The answer is simple. *Shiurim* are didactic, and if didactic methods would be all that effective, *klal Yisroel* would have done *teshuvah* long since. We have been taught *mussar* didactically from the time of the prophets onward. *Shiurim* are indeed important, but the messages in the *shiur* may not penetrate sufficiently to bring about the desired behavioral changes.

It is related that one of the great Torah scholars, who was also a wealthy merchant, was informed that one of his merchandise-laden ships had sunk at sea, and he had incurred a severe financial loss. Upon hearing the terrible news he fainted, and when his students later reminded him that he had taught them the Talmudic passage, "One must be grateful to G-d for the bad happenings as well as for the good," he responded, "I always understood that portion of the Torah *al pi drash* (theoretically), but I had not mastered it *al pi peshat* (practically)." Knowledge of a principle in the abstract does not assure its application in the concrete.

When a group of people who have each experienced the painful consequences of self-defeating behavior come together and share their experiences and look at their lives in the light of Torah teachings, this provides an opportunity for applying the theory in practice, and converting the abstract into the concrete.

We can also learn from the Twelve Step programs that involvement in a recovery program by the affected individual alone is often inadequate. People do not live in a vacuum, and they share their lives, for better or worse, with family members. The latter often become unwitting participants in the self-defeating behavior, and are therefore also in need of help for themselves.

This should not be misconstrued as an accusation that family members are responsible for the person's self-defeating behavior. The alcoholic would like everyone to believe that he drinks because his parents, wife, and children do not relate to him properly. The fact is that no one causes anyone else to drink, overeat, gamble, use drugs, overwork or lose his temper.

However, whereas family members do not *cause* the problem, they may unwittingly be accomplices to the problem, in that they do not react to the problem in an optimum manner. By analogy, oxygen is obviously not the *cause* of a fire, yet a fire cannot burn in absence of oxygen. If you deprive a flame of oxygen, it will extinguish. In many instances the family behaves in a manner that allows the self-defeating behavior to continue, hence they may be referred to as "enablers." The Talmud expresses this concept when it states, "The mouse that steals the cheese is not the thief. The thief is the mousehole which provides a haven for the mouse. If not for the mousehole, the mouse would not be there to steal" (*Gittin* 45a). Although the mousehole did not do the stealing, the Talmud holds it responsible for the theft, since it "enabled" the mouse to steal.

Earlier we alluded to the case of family members of a compulsive gambler paying his gambling debts.

This is a clear example of enabling. The same is true of the wife who bears in silence her husband's improper behavior due to alcohol, or who tells the children, "Let's be careful not to make noise. It irritates daddy." This phenomenon is also referred to as "co-dependency," which can simply be defined by saying that the person with the self-defeating behavior plays a tune, and the co-dependent family members dance to it. It is therefore necessary for family members to avoid being the enabling and protective "mousehole."

There is yet another reason why family members should be involved in a recovery program. Quite often the wife of an alcoholic will say, "The drinking is his problem. Let him go for help. I am fine, and I do not need to recover from anything." The same is true of the spouse of someone with an eating disorder.

But let us see what happens. The person with the self-defeating behavior becomes involved in a recovery program, and as we noted, this leads to elimination of various character defects and striving for greater spirituality. If the "healthy" spouse does not participate in a recovery program, it is likely that he/she will remain stagnant, fixated at a particular level, while the recovering person is engaged in personality growth and character development. After a period of time, a disparity develops between the two, which may make the relationship incompatible. If the healthy spouse undertakes a similar program for himself/herself, both can grow together and the relationship can improve.

When R' Yisroel of Salant instituted formal courses

in the study of *mussar*, he stated that this innovation was necessary because the state of morality and spirituality in the environment had deteriorated, and what was satisfactory in previous generations was not adequate now. Since the time of Rabbi Yisroel there has been a serious erosion of morality and spirituality in the world, and western civilization is in a period of unprecedented decadence. Even the regular study of *mussar* may not suffice. Rabbi Yisroel looked for ways in which the values in the *mussar* literature could be made to impact on people's emotions and behavior. We are now in even greater need of this, and perhaps the methods suggested here may contribute toward this goal.

Every person needs a recovery program, and for the Jew, that recovery program is Torah in its fullest and most comprehensive sense. As pointed out, the people who developed the Twelve Step program discovered the principles of recovery by their personal and collective experiences. Torah teachings have always contained these principles, long before the Twelve Step programs were formulated.

Implementing these Torah teachings in one's daily life can help people emerge from self-defeating lifestyles. True happiness and fulfillment of one's goal in life are not at all divergent, and it is by understanding what spirituality is and by doing all that is necessary to achieve it that we at the same time reach our goal in life, to be one with G-d, and to be the recipients of true happiness as is contained in the words of the prophet, "I will rejoice in G-d" (*Isaiah* 61:10).